Contents

Preface to the New Testame...

Introduction to Philippians...

Chapter One...7

Chapter Two...16

Chapter Three..26

Chapter Four...34

Preface to the New Testament Notes

1. For many years I have had a desire of setting down and laying together, what has occurred to my mind, either in reading, thinking, or conversation, which might assist serious persons, who have not the advantage of learning, in understanding the New Testament. But I have been continually deterred from attempting any thing of this kind, by a deep sense of my own inability: of my want, not only of learning for such a work, but much more, of experience and wisdom. This has often occasioned my laying aside the thought. And when, by much importunity, I have been prevailed upon to resume it, still I determined to delay it as long as possible, that (if it should please God) I might finish my work and my life together.

2. But having lately had a loud call from God to arise and go hence, I am convinced that if I attempt any thing of this kind at all, I must not delay any longer. My day is far spent, and (even in a natural way) the shadows of the evening come on apace. And I am the rather induced to do what little I can in this way, because I can do nothing else: being prevented, by my present weakness, from either travelling or preaching. But, blessed be God, I can still read, and write, and think. O that it may be to his glory!

3. It will be easily discerned, even from what I have said already, and much more from the notes themselves, that they were not principally designed for men of learning; who are provided with many other helps: and much less for men of long and deep experience in the ways and word of God. I desire to sit at their feet, and to learn of them. But I write chiefly for plain unlettered men, who understand only their mother tongue, and yet reverence and love the word of God, and have a desire to save their souls.

4. In order to assist these in such a measure as I am able, I

design first to set down the text itself, for the most part, in the common English translation, which is, in general, (so far as I can judge) abundantly the best that I have seen. Yet I do not say it is incapable of being brought, in several places, nearer to the original. Neither will I affirm, that the Greek copies from which this translation was made, are always the most correct. And therefore I shall take the liberty, as occasion may require, to make here and there a small alteration.

5. I am very sensible this will be liable to objections: nay, to objections of quite opposite kinds. Some will probably think, the text is altered too much; and others, that it is altered too little. To the former I would observe, that I never knowingly, so much as in one place, altered it for altering sake: but there, and there only, where first, the sense was made better, stronger, clearer, or more consistent with the context: secondly, where the sense being equally good, the phrase was better or nearer the original. To the latter, who think the alterations too few, and that the translation might have been nearer still, I answer, this is true: I acknowledge it might. But what valuable end would it have answered, to multiply such trivial alterations as add neither clearness nor strength to the text This I could not prevail upon myself to do: so much the less because there is, to my apprehension, I know not what, peculiarly solemn and venerable in the old language of our translation. And suppose this a mistaken apprehension, and an instance of human infirmity; yet, is it not an excusable infirmity, to be unwilling to part with what we have been long accustomed to; and to love the very words by which God has often conveyed strength or comfort to our souls!

6. I have endeavoured to make the notes as short as possible that the comment may not obscure or swallow up the text: and as plain as possible, in pursuance of my main design, to assist the unlearned reader: for this reason I have studiously avoided, not only all curious and critical inquiries, and all use of the learned languages, but all such methods of reasoning

and modes of expression as people in common life are unacquainted with: for the same reason, as I rather endeavour to obviate than to propose and answer questions, so I purposely decline going deep into many difficulties, lest I should leave the ordinary reader behind me.

7. I once designed to write down barely what occurred, to my own mind, consulting none but the inspired writers. But no sooner was I acquainted with that great light of the Christian world, (lately gone to his reward,) Bengelius, than I entirely changed my design, being thoroughly convinced it might be of more service to the cause of religion, were I barely to translate his Gnomon Novi Testamenti, than to write many volumes upon it. Many of his excellent notes I have therefore translated. Many more I have abridged, omitting that part which was purely critical, and giving the substance of the rest. Those various readings likewise, which he has showed to have a vast majority of ancient copies and translations on their side, I have without scruple incorporated with the text; which, after his manner, I have divided all along (though not omitting the common division into chapters and verses, which is of use on various accounts) according to the matter it contains, making a larger or smaller pause, just as the sense requires. And even this is such a help in many places, as one who has not tried it can scarcely conceive.

8. I am likewise indebted for some useful observations to Dr. Heylin's Theological Lectures: and for many more to Dr. Guyse, and to the Family Expositor of the late pious and learned Dr. Doddridge It was a doubt with me for some time, whether I should not subjoin to every note I received from them the name of the author from whom it was taken; especially considering I had transcribed some, and abridged many more, almost in the words of the author. But upon farther consideration, I resolved to name none, that nothing might divert the mind of the reader from keeping close to the point in view, and receiving what was spoken only according

to its own intrinsic value.

9. I cannot flatter myself so far (to use the words of one of the above - named writers) as to imagine that I have fallen into no mistakes in a work of so great difficulty. But my own conscience acquits me of having designedly misrepresented any single passage of Scripture, or of having written one line with a purpose of inflaming the hearts of Christians against each other. God forbid that I should make the words of the most gentle and benevolent Jesus a vehicle to convey such poison. Would to God that all the party names, and unscriptural phrases and forms, which have divided the Christian world, were forgot: and that we might all agree to sit down together, as humble, loving disciples, at the feet of our common Master, to hear his word, to imbibe his Spirit, and to transcribe his life in our own!

10. Concerning the Scriptures in general, it may be observed, the word of the living God, which directed the first patriarchs also, was, in the time of Moses, committed to writing. To this were added, in several succeeding generations, the inspired writings of the other prophets. Afterward, what the Son of God preached, and the Holy Ghost spake by the apostles, the apostles and evangelists wrote. - This is what we now style the Holy Scripture: this is that word of God which remaineth for ever: of which, though heaven and earth pass away, one jot or tittle shall not pass away. The Scripture therefore of the Old and New Testament, is a most solid and precious system of Divine truth. Every part thereof is worthy of God; and all together are one entire body, wherein is no defect, no excess. It is the fountain of heavenly wisdom, which they who are able to taste, prefer to all writings of men, however wise, or learned, or holy.

11. An exact knowledge of the truth was accompanied in the inspired writers with an exactly regular series of arguments, a precise expression of their meaning, and a genuine vigour of

suitable affections. The chain of argument in each book is briefly exhibited in the table prefixed to it, which contains also the sum thereof, and may be of more use than prefixing the argument to each chapter; the division of the New Testament into chapters having been made in the dark ages, and very incorrectly; often separating things that are closely joined, and joining those that are entirely distinct from each other.

12. In the language of the sacred writings, we may observe the utmost depth, together with the utmost ease. All the elegancies of human composures sink into nothing before it: God speaks not as man, but as God. His thoughts are very deep: and thence his words are of inexhaustible virtue. And the language of his messengers also is exact in the highest degree: for the words which were given them accurately answered the impression made upon their minds: and hence Luther says, "Divinity is nothing but a grammar of the language of the Holy Ghost." To understand this thoroughly, we should observe the emphasis which lies on every word; the holy affections expressed thereby, and the tempers shown by every writer. But how little are these, the latter especially, regarded Though they are wonderfully diffused through the whole New Testament, and are in truth a continued commendation of him who acts, or speaks, or writes.

13. The New Testament is all those sacred writings in which the New Testament or covenant is described. The former part of this contains the writings of the evangelists and apostles: the latter, the revelation of Jesus Christ. In the former is, first, the history of Jesus Christ, from his coming in the flesh to his ascension into heaven; then the institution and history of the Christian Church, from the time of his ascension. The revelation delivers what is to be, with regard to Christ, the Church, and the universe, till the consummation of all things.
BRISTOL HOT-WELLS,
January 4, 1754.

Introduction to Philippians

PHILIPPI was so called from Philip, king of Macedonia, who much enlarged and beautified it. Afterwards it became a Roman colony, and the chief city of that part of Macedonia. Hither St. Paul was sent by a vision to preach and here, not long after his coming, he was shamefully entreated. Nevertheless many were converted by him, during the short time of his abode there; by whose liberality he was more assisted than by any other church of his planting. And they had now sent large assistance to him by Epaphroditus; by whom he returns them this epistle.

It contains six parts:

I. The inscription - C.i. 1,2

II. Thanksgiving and prayers for them - 3-11

III.He relates his present state and good hope - 12-24
Whence he exhorts them,
1. While he remains with them to walk worthy of the gospel - 25-30 C. ii. 1-16
2. Though he should be killed, to rejoice with him - 17,18
And promises,
1. To certify them of all things by Timotheus - 19-24
2. In the mean time to send Epaphroditus - 25-30

IV. He exhorts them to rejoice - C. iii. 1-3
admonishing them to beware of false teachers, and to imitate the true - 2-21
commending concord - C. iv. 1-3
He again exhorts them to joy and meekness - 4-7
and to whatsoever things are excellent - 8-9

V. He accepts of their liberality - 10-20
VI. The conclusion – 21-23

Chapter One

Verse 1

1 Paul and Timotheus, the servants of Jesus Christ, to all the saints in Christ Jesus which are at Philippi, with the bishops and deacons:

Servants — St. Paul, writing familiarly to the Philippians, does not style himself an apostle. And under the common title of servants, he tenderly and modestly joins with himself his son Timotheus, who had come to Philippi not long after St. Paul had received him, Acts 16:3,12.

To all the saints — The apostolic epistles were sent more directly to the churches, than to the pastors of them.

With the bishops and deacons — The former properly took care of the internal state, the latter, of the externals, of the church, 1 Timothy 3:2-8; although these were not wholly confined to the one, neither those to the other. The word bishops here includes all the presbyters at Philippi, as well as the ruling presbyters: the names bishop and presbyter, or elder, being promiscuously used in the first ages.

Verse 4

4 Always in every prayer of mine for you all making request with joy,

Joy

With joy — After the epistle to the Ephesians, wherein love reigns, follows this, wherein there is perpetual mention of joy. "The fruit of the Spirit is love, joy." And joy peculiarly enlivens prayer. The sum of the whole epistle is, I rejoice. Rejoice ye.

Verse 5

5 For your fellowship in the gospel from the first day until now;

The sense is, I thank God for your fellowship with us in all the blessings of the gospel, which I have done from the first day of your receiving it until now.

Verse 6

6 Being confident of this very thing, that he which hath begun a good work in you will perform it until the day of Jesus Christ:

Being persuaded — The grounds of which persuasion are set down in the following verse.

That he who hath begun a good work in you, will perfect it until the day of Christ — That he who having justified, hath begun to sanctify you, will carry on this work, till it issue in glory.

Verse 7

7 Even as it is meet for me to think this of you all, because I have you in my heart; inasmuch as both in my bonds, and in the defence and confirmation of the gospel, ye all are partakers of my grace.

As it is right for me to think this of you all — Why? He does not say, "Because of an eternal decree;" or, "Because a saint must persevere;" but, because I have you in my heart, who were all partakers of my grace - That is, because ye were all (for which I have you in my heart, I bear you the most grateful and tender affection) partakers of my grace - That is, sharers in the afflictions which God vouchsafed me as a grace or favour, Philippians 1:29,30; both in my bonds, and when I was called forth to answer for myself, and to confirm the gospel. It is not improbable that, after they had endured that great trial of affliction, God had sealed them unto full victory, of which the apostle had a prophetic sight.

Verse 8

8 For God is my record, how greatly I long after you all in the bowels of Jesus Christ.

I long for you with the bowels of Jesus Christ — In Paul, not Paul lives, but Jesus Christ. Therefore he longs for them with the bowels, the tenderness, not of Paul, but of Jesus Christ.

Verse 9

9 And this I pray, that your love may abound yet more and more in knowledge and in all judgment;

And this I pray, that your love — Which they had already shown.

May abound yet more and more — The fire which burned in the apostle never says, It is enough.

In knowledge and in all spiritual sense — Which is the ground of all spiritual knowledge. We must be inwardly sensible of divine peace, joy, love; otherwise, we cannot know what they are.

Verse 10

10 That ye may approve things that are excellent; that ye may be sincere and without offence till the day of Christ;

That ye may try — By that spiritual sense.

The things that are excellent — Not only good, but the very best; the superior excellence of which is hardly discerned, but by the adult Christian. That ye may be inwardly sincere - Having a single eye to the very best things, and a pure heart. And outwardly without offence - Holy, unblamable in all things.

Verse 11

11 Being filled with the fruits of righteousness, which are by Jesus Christ, unto the glory and praise of God.

Being filled with the fruits of righteousness, which are through Jesus Christ, to the glory and praise of God — Here are three properties of that sincerity which is acceptable to God: 1. It must bear fruits, the fruits of righteousness, all inward and outward holiness, all good tempers, words, and works; and that so abundantly, that we may be filled with them. 2. The branch and the fruits must derive both their virtue and their very being from the all - supporting, all - supplying root, Jesus Christ. 3. As all these flow from the grace of Christ, so they must issue in the glory and praise of God.

Verse 12

12 But I would ye should understand, brethren, that the things which happened unto me have fallen out rather unto the furtherance of the gospel;

The things concerning me — My sufferings. Have fallen out rather to the furtherance, than, as you feared, the hinderance, of the gospel.

Verse 13

13 So that my bonds in Christ are manifest in all the palace, and in all other places;

My bonds in Christ — Endured for his sake.

Have been made manifest — Much taken notice of.

In the whole palace — Of the Roman emperor.

Verse 14

14 And many of the brethren in the Lord, waxing confident by my bonds, are much more bold to speak the word without fear.

And many — Who were before afraid.

Trusting in the Lord through my bonds — When they observed my constancy, and safety not withstanding, are more bold.

Verses 15-16

15 Some indeed preach Christ even of envy and strife; and some also of good will: 16 The one preach Christ of contention, not sincerely, supposing to add affliction to my bonds:

Some indeed preach Christ out of contention — Envying St. Paul's success, and striving to hurt him thereby.

Not sincerely — From a real desire to glorify God.

But supposing — Though they were disappointed. To add more affliction to my bonds - By enraging the Romans against me.

Verse 17

17 But the other of love, knowing that I am set for the defence of the gospel.

But the others out of love — To Christ and me.

Knowing — Not barely, supposing.

That I am set — Literally, I lie; yet still going forward in his work. He remained at Rome as an ambassador in a place where he is employed on an important embassy.

Verse 18

18 What then? notwithstanding, every way, whether in pretence, or in truth, Christ is preached; and I therein do rejoice, yea, and will rejoice.

In pretence — Under colour of propagating the gospel.

In truth — With a real design so to do.

Verse 19

19 For I know that this shall turn to my salvation through your prayer, and the supply of the Spirit of Jesus Christ,

This shall turn to my salvation — Shall procure me an higher degree of glory.

Through your prayer — Obtaining for me a larger supply of the Spirit.

Verse 20

20 According to my earnest expectation and my hope, that in nothing I shall be ashamed, but that with all boldness, as always, so now also Christ shall be magnified in my body, whether it be by life, or by death.

As always — Since my call to the apostleship.

In my body — however it may he disposed of. How that might be, he did not yet know. For the apostles did not know all things; particularly in things pertaining to themselves, they had room to exercise faith and patience.

Verse 21

21 For to me to live is Christ, and to die is gain.

To me to live is Christ — To know, to love, to follow Christ, is my life, my glory, my joy.

Verse 22

22 But if I live in the flesh, this is the fruit of my labour: yet what I shall choose I wot not.

Here he begins to treat of the former clause of the preceding verse. Of the latter he treats, Philippians 2:17.

But if I am to live is the flesh, this is the fruit of my labour — This is the fruit of my living longer, that I can labour more. Glorious labour! desirable fruit! in this view, long life is indeed a blessing.

And what I should choose I know not — That is, if it were left to my choice.

Verse 23

23 For I am in a strait betwixt two, having a desire to depart, and to be with Christ; which is far better:

To depart — Out of bonds, flesh, the world.

And to be with Christ — In a nearer and fuller union. It is better to depart; it is far better to be with Christ.

Verse 25

25 And having this confidence, I know that I shall abide and continue with you all for your furtherance and joy of faith;

I know — By a prophetic notice given him while he was writing this. That I shall continue some time longer with you - And doubtless he did see them after this confinement.

Verse 27

27 Only let your conversation be as it becometh the gospel of Christ: that whether I come and see you, or else be absent, I may hear of your affairs, that ye stand fast in one spirit, with one mind striving together for the faith of the gospel;

Only — Be careful for this, and nothing else.

Stand fast in one spirit — With the most perfect unanimity.

Striving together — With united strength and endeavours.

For the faith of the gospel — For all the blessings revealed and promised therein.

Verse 28

28 And in nothing terrified by your adversaries: which is to them an evident token of perdition, but to you of salvation, and that of God.

Which — Namely, their being adversaries to the word of God, and to you the messengers of God.

Is an evident token — That they are in the high road to perdition; and you, in the way of salvation.

Verse 29

29 For unto you it is given in the behalf of Christ, not only to believe on him, but also to suffer for his sake;

For to you it is given — As a special token of God's love, and of your being in the way of salvation.

Verse 30

30 Having the same conflict which ye saw in me, and now hear to be in me.

Having the same kind of conflict with your adversaries, which ye saw in me - When I was with you, Acts 16:12,19, etc.

Chapter Two

Verse 1

1 If there be therefore any consolation in Christ, if any comfort of love, if any fellowship of the Spirit, if any bowels and mercies,

If there be therefore any consolation — In the grace of Christ.

If any comfort — In the love of God. If any fellowship of the Holy Ghost; if any bowels of mercies - Resulting therefrom; any tender affection towards each other.

Verse 2

2 Fulfil ye my joy, that ye be likeminded, having the same love, being of one accord, of one mind.

Think the same thing — Seeing Christ is your common Head.

Having the same love — To God, your common Father.

Being of one soul — Animated with the same affections and tempers, as ye have all drank ill to one spirit.

Of one mind — Tenderly rejoicing and grieving together.

Verse 3

3 Let nothing be done through strife or vainglory; but in lowliness of mind let each esteem other better than themselves.

Do nothing through contention — Which is inconsistent with your thinking the same thing.

Or vainglory — Desire of praise, which is directly opposite to the love of God.

But esteem each the others better than themselves — (For every one knows more evil of himself than he can of another:) Which is a glorious fruit of the Spirit, and an admirable help to your continuing "of one soul."

Verse 4

4 Look not every man on his own things, but every man also on the things of others.

Aim not every one at his own things — Only. If so, ye have not bowels of mercies.

Verse 6

6 Who, being in the form of God, thought it not robbery to be equal with God:

Who being in the essential form — The incommunicable nature.

Of God — From eternity, as he was afterward in the form of man; real God, as real man.

Counted it no act of robbery — That is the precise meaning of the words,-no invasion of another's prerogative, but his own strict and unquestionable right.

To be equal with God — the word here translated equal, occurs in the adjective form five or six times in the New Testament, Matthew 20:12; Luke 6:34; John 5:18; Acts 11:17; Revelation 21:16. In all which places it expresses not a bare resemblance, but a real and proper equality. It here implies both the fulness and the supreme height of the

Godhead; to which are opposed, he emptied and he humbled himself.

Verse 7

7 But made himself of no reputation, and took upon him the form of a servant, and was made in the likeness of men:

Yet — He was so far from tenaciously insisting upon, that he willingly relinquished, his claim. He was content to forego the glories of the Creator, and to appear in the form of a creature; nay, to he made in the likeness of the fallen creatures; and not only to share the disgrace, but to suffer the punishment, due to the meanest and vilest among them all.

He emptied himself — Of that divine fulness, which he received again at his exaltation. Though he remained full, John 1:14, yet he appeared as if he had been empty; for he veiled his fulness from the sight of men and angels. Yea, he not only veiled, but, in some sense, renounced, the glory which he had before the world began.

Taking — And by that very act emptying himself.

The form of a servant — The form, the likeness, the fashion, though not exactly the same, are yet nearly related to each other. The form expresses something absolute; the likeness refers to other things of the same kind; the fashion respects what appears to sight and sense.

Being made in the likeness of men — A real man, like other men. Hereby he took the form of a servant.

Verse 8

8 And being found in fashion as a man, he humbled himself, and became obedient unto death, even the death of the cross.

And being found in fashion as a man — A common man, without any peculiar excellence or comeliness.

He humbled himself — To a still greater depth.

Becoming obedient — To God, though equal with him.

Even unto death — The greatest instance both of humiliation and obedience.

Yea, the death of the cross — Inflicted on few but servants or slaves.

Verse 9

9 Wherefore God also hath highly exalted him, and given him a name which is above every name:

Wherefore — Because of his voluntary humiliation and obedience. He humbled himself; but God hath exalted him - So recompensing his humiliation.

And hath given him — So recompensing his emptying himself.

A name which is above every name — Dignity and majesty superior to every creature.

Verse 10

10 That at the name of Jesus every knee should bow, of things in heaven, and things in earth, and things under the earth;

That every knee — That divine honour might be paid in every possible manner by every creature.

Might bow — Either with love or trembling.

Of those in heaven, earth, under the earth — That is, through the whole universe.

Verse 11

11 And that every tongue should confess that Jesus Christ is Lord, to the glory of God the Father.

And every tongue — Even of his enemies.

Confess that Jesus Christ is Lord — Jehovah; not now "in the form of a servant," but enthroned in the glory of God the Father.

Verse 12

12 Wherefore, my beloved, as ye have always obeyed, not as in my presence only, but now much more in my absence, work out your own salvation with fear and trembling.

Wherefore — Having proposed Christ's example, he exhorts them to secure the salvation which Christ has purchased.

As ye have always — Hitherto.

Obeyed — Both God, and me his minister.

Now in my absence — When ye have not me to instruct, assist, and direct you.

Work out your own salvation — Herein let every man aim at his own things.

With fear and trembling — With the utmost care and diligence.

Verse 13

13 For it is God which worketh in you both to will and to do of his good pleasure.

For it is God — God alone, who is with you, though I am not.

That worketh in you according to his good pleasure — Not for any merit of yours. Yet his influences are not to supersede, but to encourage, our own efforts.

Work out your own salvation — Here is our duty.

For it is God that worketh in you — Here is our encouragement. And O, what a glorious encouragement, to have the arm of Omnipotence stretched out for our support and our succour!

Verse 14

14 Do all things without murmurings and disputings:

Do all things — Not only without contention, Philippians 2:3, but even without murmurings and disputings - Which are real, though smaller, hinderances of love.

Verse 15

15 That ye may be blameless and harmless, the sons of God, without rebuke, in the midst of a crooked and perverse nation, among whom ye shine as lights in the world;

That ye may be blameless — Before men.

And simple — Before God, aiming at him alone.

As the sons of God — The God of love; acting up to your

high character.

Unrebukable in the midst of a crooked — Guileful, serpentine, and perverse generation - Such as the bulk of mankind always were.

Crooked — By a corrupt nature, and yet more perverse by custom and practice.

Verse 17

17 Yea, and if I be offered upon the sacrifice and service of your faith, I joy, and rejoice with you all.

Here he begins to treat of the latter clause of Philippians 1:22.

Yea, and if I be offered — Literally, If I be poured out.

Upon the sacrifice of your faith — The Philippians, as the other converted heathens, were a sacrifice to God through St. Paul's ministry, Romans 15:16. And as in sacrificing, wine was poured at the foot of the altar, so he was willing that his blood should be poured out. The expression well agrees with that kind of martyrdom by which he was afterwards offered up to God.

Verse 18

18 For the same cause also do ye joy, and rejoice with me.

Congratulate me — When I am offered up.

Verse 19

19 But I trust in the Lord Jesus to send Timotheus shortly unto you, that I also may be of good comfort, when I know your state.

When I know — Upon my return, that ye stand steadfast.

Verse 20

20 For I have no man likeminded, who will naturally care for your state.

I have none — Of those who are now with me.

Verse 21

21 For all seek their own, not the things which are Jesus Christ's.

For all — But Timotheus.

Seek their own — Ease, safety, pleasure, or profit. Amazing! In that golden age of the church, could St. Paul throughly approve of one only, among all the labourers that were with him? Philippians 1:14,17. And how many do we think can now approve themselves to God? Not the things of Jesus Christ - They who seek these alone, will sadly experience this. They will find few helpers likeminded with themselves, willing naked to follow a naked Master.

Verse 22

22 But ye know the proof of him, that, as a son with the father, he hath served with me in the gospel.

As a son with his father — He uses an elegant peculiarity of phrase, speaking partly as of a son, partly as of a fellowlabourer.

Verse 25

25 Yet I supposed it necessary to send to you Epaphroditus, my brother, and companion in labour, and fellowsoldier, but your messenger, and he that ministered to my wants.

To send Epaphroditus — Back immediately.

Your messenger — The Philippians had sent him to St. Paul with their liberal contribution.

Verse 26

26 For he longed after you all, and was full of heaviness, because that ye had heard that he had been sick.

He was full of heaviness — Because he supposed you would be afflicted at hearing that he was sick.

Verse 27

27 For indeed he was sick nigh unto death: but God had mercy on him; and not on him only, but on me also, lest I should have sorrow upon sorrow.

God had compassion on him — Restoring him to health.

Verse 28

28 I sent him therefore the more carefully, that, when ye see him again, ye may rejoice, and that I may be the less sorrowful.

That I may be the less sorrowful — When I know you are rejoicing.

Verse 30

30 Because for the work of Christ he was nigh unto death, not regarding his life, to supply your lack of service toward me.

To supply your deficiency of service — To do what you could not do in person.

Chapter Three

Verse 1

1 Finally, my brethren, rejoice in the Lord. To write the same things to you, to me indeed is not grievous, but for you it is safe.

The same things — Which you have heard before.

Verse 2

2 Beware of dogs, beware of evil workers, beware of the concision.

Beware of dogs — Unclean, unholy, rapacious men. The title which the Jews usually gave the gentiles, he returns upon themselves.

The concision — Circumcision being now ceased, the apostle will not call them the circumcision, but coins a term on purpose, taken from a Greek word used by the LXX, Leviticus 21:5, for such a cutting as God had forbidden.

Verse 3

3 For we are the circumcision, which worship God in the spirit, and rejoice in Christ Jesus, and have no confidence in the flesh.

For we — Christians. Are the only true circumcision - The people now in covenant with God.

Who worship God in spirit — Not barely in the letter, but with the spiritual worship of inward holiness.

And glory in Christ Jesus — As the only cause of all our

blessings.

And have no confidence in the flesh — In any outward advantage or prerogative.

Verse 4

4 Though I might also have confidence in the flesh. If any other man thinketh that he hath whereof he might trust in the flesh, I more:

Though I — He subjoins this in the singular number, because the Philippians could not say thus.

Verse 5

5 Circumcised the eighth day, of the stock of Israel, of the tribe of Benjamin, an Hebrew of the Hebrews; as touching the law, a Pharisee;

Circumcised the eighth day — Not at ripe age, as a proselyte.

Of the tribe of Benjamin — Sprung from the wife, not the handmaid.

An Hebrew of Hebrews — By both my parents; in everything, nation, religion, language.

Touching the law, a pharisee — One of that sect who most accurately observe it.

Verse 6

5 Concerning zeal, persecuting the church; touching the righteousness which is in the law, blameless.

Having such a zeal for it as to persecute to the death those who did not observe it. Touching the righteousness which is described and enjoined by the Law - That is, external observances, blameless.

Verse 7

7 But what things were gain to me, those I counted loss for Christ.

But all these things, which I then accounted gain, which were once my confidence, my glory, and joy, those, ever since I have believed, I have accounted loss, nothing worth in comparison of Christ.

Verse 8

8 Yea doubtless, and I count all things but loss for the excellency of the knowledge of Christ Jesus my Lord: for whom I have suffered the loss of all things, and do count them but dung, that I may win Christ,

Yea, I still account both all these and all things else to be mere loss, compared to the inward, experimental knowledge of Christ, as my Lord, as my prophet, priest, and king, as teaching me wisdom, atoning for my sins, and reigning in my heart. To refer this to justification only, is miserably to pervert the whole scope of the words. They manifestly relate to sanctification also; yea, to that chiefly. For whom I have actually suffered the loss of all things - Which the world loves, esteems, or admires; of which I am so far from repenting, that I still account them but dung - The discourse rises. Loss is sustained with patience, but dung is cast away with abhorrence. The Greek word signifies any, the vilest refuse of things, the dross of metals, the dregs of liquors, the excrements of animals, the most worthless scraps of meat, the basest offals, fit only for dogs.

That I may gain Christ — He that loses all things, not excepting himself, gains Christ, and is gained by Christ. And still there is more; which even St. Paul speaks of his having not yet gained.

Verse 9

9 And be found in him, not having mine own righteousness, which is of the law, but that which is through the faith of Christ, the righteousness which is of God by faith:

And be found by God ingrafted in him, not having my own righteousness, which is of the law - That merely outward righteousness prescribed by the law, and performed by my own strength. But that inward righteousness which is through faith - Which can flow from no other fountain.

The righteousness which is from God — From his almighty Spirit, not by my own strength, but by faith alone. Here also the apostle is far from speaking of justification only.

Verse 10

10 That I may know him, and the power of his resurrection, and the fellowship of his sufferings, being made conformable unto his death;

The knowledge of Christ, mentioned in the eighth verse, is here more largely explained.

That I may know him — As my complete Saviour.

And the power of his resurrection — Raising me from the death of sin, into all the life of love.

And the fellowship of his sufferings — Being crucified with him.

And made conformable to his death — So as to be dead to all things here below.

Verse 11

11 If by any means I might attain unto the resurrection of the dead.

The resurrection of the dead — That is, the resurrection to glory.

Verse 12

12 Not as though I had already attained, either were already perfect: but I follow after, if that I may apprehend that for which also I am apprehended of Christ Jesus.

Not that I have already attained — The prize. He here enters on a new set of metaphors, taken from a race. But observe how, in the utmost fervour, he retains his sobriety of spirit.

Or am already perfected — There is a difference between one that is perfect, and one that is perfected. The one is fitted for the race, Philippians 3:15; the other, ready to receive the prize.

But I pursue, if I may apprehend that — Perfect holiness, preparatory to glory. For, in order to which I was apprehended by Christ Jesus - Appearing to me in the way, Acts 26:14. The speaking conditionally both here and in the preceding verse, implies no uncertainty, but only the difficulty of attaining.

Verse 13

13 Brethren, I count not myself to have apprehended: but this one thing I do, forgetting those things which are behind, and reaching forth unto those things which are before,

I do not account myself to have apprehended this already; to be already possessed of perfect holiness.

Verse 14

14 I press toward the mark for the prize of the high calling of God in Christ Jesus.

Forgetting the things that are behind — Even that part of the race which is already run.

And reaching forth unto — Literally, stretched out over the things that are before - Pursuing with the whole bent and vigour of my soul, perfect holiness and eternal glory.

In Christ Jesus — The author and finisher of every good thing.

Verse 15

15 Let us therefore, as many as be perfect, be thus minded: and if in any thing ye be otherwise minded, God shall reveal even this unto you.

Let us, as many as are perfect — Fit for the race, strong in faith; so it means here.

Be thus minded — Apply wholly to this one thing.

And if in anything ye — Who are not perfect, who are weak in faith.

Be otherwise minded — Pursuing other things. God, if ye desire it, shall reveal even this unto you - Will convince you of it.

Verse 16

16 Nevertheless, whereto we have already attained, let us walk by the same rule, let us mind the same thing.

But let us take care not to lose the ground we have already gained. Let us walk by the same rule we have done hitherto.

Verse 17

17 Brethren, be followers together of me, and mark them which walk so as ye have us for an ensample.

Mark them — For your imitation.

Verse 18

18 (For many walk, of whom I have told you often, and now tell you even weeping, that they are the enemies of the cross of Christ:

Weeping — As he wrote.

Enemies of the cross of Christ — Such are all cowardly, all shamefaced, all delicate Christians.

Verse 19

19 Whose end is destruction, whose God is their belly, and whose glory is in their shame, who mind earthly things.)

Whose end is destruction — This is placed in the front, that what follows may be read with the greater horror.

Whose god is their belly — Whose supreme happiness lies in gratifying their sensual appetites.

Who mind — Relish, desire, seek, earthly things.

Verse 20

20 For our conversation is in heaven; from whence also we look for the Saviour, the Lord Jesus Christ:

Our conversation — The Greek word is of a very extensive meaning: our citizenship, our thoughts, our affections, are already in heaven.

Verse 21

21 Who shall change our vile body, that it may be fashioned like unto his glorious body, according to the working whereby he is able even to subdue all things unto himself.

Who will transform our vile body — Into the most perfect state, and the most beauteous form. It will then be purer than the unspotted firmament, brighter than the lustre of the stars and, which exceeds all parallel, which comprehends all perfection, like unto his glorious body - Like that wonderfully glorious body which he wears in his heavenly kingdom, and on his triumphant throne.

Chapter Four

Verse 1

1 Therefore, my brethren dearly beloved and longed for, my joy and crown, so stand fast in the Lord, my dearly beloved.

So stand — As ye have done hitherto.

Verse 2

2 I beseech Euodias, and beseech Syntyche, that they be of the same mind in the Lord.

I beseech — He repeats this twice, as if speaking to each face to face, and that with the utmost tenderness.

Verse 3

3 And I intreat thee also, true yokefellow, help those women which laboured with me in the gospel, with Clement also, and with other my fellowlabourers, whose names are in the book of life.

And I entreat thee also, true yokefellow — St. Paul had many fellowlabourers, but not many yokefellows. In this number was Barnabas first, and then Silas, whom he probably addresses here; for Silas had been his yokefellow at the very place, Acts 16:19.

Help those women who laboured together with me — Literally, who wrestled. The Greek word doth not imply preaching, or anything of that kind; but danger and toil endured for the sake of the gospel, which was also endured at the same time, probably at Philippi, by Clement and my other fellowlabourers - This is a different word from the former, and does properly imply fellowpreachers. Whose names, although not set down here, are in the book of life - As are those of all believers. An allusion to the wrestlers in the Olympic games, whose names were all enrolled in a book. Reader, is thy name there? Then walk circumspectly, lest the Lord blot thee out of his book!

Verse 5

5 Let your moderation be known unto all men. The Lord is at hand.

Let your gentleness — Yieldingness, sweetness of temper, the result of joy in the Lord.

Be known — By your whole behaviour.

To all men — Good and bad, gentle and froward. Those of the roughest tempers are good natured to some, from natural sympathy and various motives; a Christian, to all.

The Lord — The judge, the rewarder, the avenger.

Is at hand — Standeth at the door.

Verse 6

6 Be careful for nothing; but in every thing by prayer and supplication with thanksgiving let your requests be made known unto God.

Be anxiously careful for nothing - If men are not gentle towards you, yet neither on this, nor any other account, be careful, but pray. Carefulness and prayer cannot stand together.

In every thing — Great and small.

Let your requests be made known — They who by a preposterous shame or distrustful modesty, cover, stifle, or keep in their desires, as if they were either too small or too great, must be racked with care; from which they are entirely delivered, who pour them out with a free and filial confidence.

To God — It is not always proper to disclose them to men.

By supplication — Which is the enlarging upon and pressing our petition.

With thanksgiving — The surest mark of a soul free from care, and of prayer joined with true resignation. This is always followed by peace. Peace and thanksgiving are both coupled together, Colossians 3:15.

Verse 7

7 And the peace of God, which passeth all understanding, shall keep your hearts and minds through Christ Jesus.

And the peace of God — That calm, heavenly repose, that tranquility of spirit, which God only can give.

Which surpasseth all understanding — Which none can comprehend, save he that receiveth it.

Shall keep — Shall guard, as a garrison does a city.

Your hearts — Your affections.

Your minds — Your understandings, and all the various workings of them; through the Spirit and power of Christ Jesus, in the knowledge and love of God. Without a guard set on these likewise, the purity and vigour of our affections cannot long be preserved.

Verse 8

8 Finally, brethren, whatsoever things are true, whatsoever things are honest, whatsoever things are just, whatsoever things are pure, whatsoever things are lovely, whatsoever things are of good report; if there be any virtue, and if there be any praise, think on these things.

Finally — To sum up all.

Whatsoever things are true — Here are eight particulars placed in two fourfold rows; the former containing their duty; the latter, the commendation of it. The first word in the former row answers the first in the latter; the second word, the second and so on.

True — In speech.

Honest — In action.

Just — With regard to others.

Pure — With regard to yourselves.

Lovely — And what more lovely than truth? Of good report - As is honesty, even where it is not practised.

If there be any virtue — And all virtues are contained in justice.

If there be any praise — In those things which relate rather to ourselves than to our neighbour.

Think on these things — That ye may both practise them yourselves, and recommend them to others.

Verse 9

9 Those things, which ye have both learned, and received, and heard, and seen in me, do: and the God of peace shall be with you.

The things which ye have learned — As catechumens.

And received — By continual instructions.

And heard and seen — In my life and conversation.

These do, and the God of peace shall be with you — Not only the peace of God, but God himself, the fountain of peace.

Verse 10

10 But I rejoiced in the Lord greatly, that now at the last your care of me hath flourished again; wherein ye were also careful, but ye lacked opportunity.

I rejoiced greatly — St. Paul was no Stoic: he had strong passions, but all devoted to God.

That your care of me hath flourished again — As a tree blossoms after the winter.

Ye wanted opportunity — Either ye had not plenty yourselves, or you wanted a proper messenger.

Verse 11

11 Not that I speak in respect of want: for I have learned, in whatsoever state I am, therewith to be content.

I have learned — From God. He only can teach this.

In everything, therewith to be content — Joyfully and thankfully patient. Nothing less is Christian content. We may observe a beautiful gradation in the expressions, I have learned; I know; I am instructed; I can.

Verse 12

12 I know both how to be abased, and I know how to abound: every where and in all things I am instructed both to be full and to be hungry, both to abound and to suffer need.

I know how to be abased — Having scarce what is needful for my body.

And to abound — Having wherewith to relieve others also. Presently after, the order of the words is inverted, to intimate his frequent transition from scarcity to plenty, and from plenty to scarcity.

I am instructed — Literally, I am initiated in that mystery, unknown to all but Christians.

Both to be full and to be hungry — For one day.

Both to abound and to want — For a longer season.

Verse 13

13 I can do all things through Christ which strengtheneth me.

I can do all things — Even fulfil all the will of God.

Verse 15

15 Now ye Philippians know also, that in the beginning of the gospel, when I departed from Macedonia, no church communicated with me as concerning giving and receiving, but ye only.

In the beginning of the gospel — When it was first preached at Philippi.

In respect of giving — On your part.

And receiving — On mine.

Verse 17

17 Not because I desire a gift: but I desire fruit that may abound to your account.

Not that I desire — For my own sake, the very gift which I receive of you.

Verse 18

18 But I have all, and abound: I am full, having received of Epaphroditus the things which were sent from you, an odour of a sweet smell, a sacrifice acceptable, wellpleasing to God.

An odour of a sweet smell — More pleasing to God than the sweetest perfumes to men.

Verse 19

19 But my God shall supply all your need according to his riches in glory by Christ Jesus.

All your need — As ye have mine.

According to his riches in glory — In his abundant, eternal glory.

29140188R00027

Printed in Great Britain
by Amazon